the Veggie
salad bowl

the *Veggie* salad bowl

MORE THAN 60 DELICIOUS VEGETARIAN AND VEGAN RECIPES

RYLAND PETERS & SMALL
LONDON • NEW YORK

Senior designer Toni Kay
Editor Miriam Catley
Head of Production
  Patricia Harrington
Art director Leslie Harrington
Editorial director Julia Charles
Publisher Cindy Richards

First published in 2018 by
Ryland Peters & Small
20–21 Jockey's Fields, London
WC1R 4BW
and
341 E 116th St, New York
NY 10029
www.rylandpeters.com

10 9 8 7 6 5 4 3 2 1

Recipe collection compiled by
Julia Charles. Text copyright ©
Jordan Bourke, Chloe Coker and
Jane Montgomery, Ursula Ferrigno,
Amy Ruth Finegold, Mat Follas,
Acland Geddes, Dunja Gulin, Vicky
Jones, Jenny Linford, Rosa Rigby
and Ryland Peters & Small 2018
Design and photographs copyright
© Ryland Peters & Small 2018

ISBN: 978-1-84975-965-6

Printed in China

A CIP record for this book is available
from the British Library.

US Library of Congress
Cataloging-in-Publication Data
has been applied for.

NOTES:
• Both British (Metric) and
American (Imperial plus US cups)
measurements are included in
 these recipes for your convenience,
however it is important to work
with one set of measurements
and not alternate between the
two within a recipe.

• All spoon measurements are level
unless otherwise specified.
• All eggs are medium (UK) or large
(US), unless specified as large, in
which case US extra-large should
be used. Uncooked or partially
cooked eggs should not be served
to the very old, frail, young children,
pregnant women or those with
compromised immune systems.
• Ovens should be preheated
 to the specified temperatures.
We recommend using an oven
thermometer. If using a fan-assisted
oven, adjust temperatures according
to the manufacturer's instructions.
• When a recipe calls for the grated
zest of citrus fruit, buy unwaxed fruit
and wash well before using. If you
can only find treated fruit, scrub well
in warm soapy water before using.
• To sterilize preserving jars, wash
them in hot, soapy water and rinse
in boiling water. Place in a large
saucepan and cover with hot water.
With the saucepan lid on, bring the
water to a boil and continue boiling
for 15 minutes. Turn off the heat and
leave the jars in the hot water until
just before they are to be filled.
Invert the jars onto a clean kitchen
cloth to dry. Sterilize the lids for
5 minutes, by boiling or according
to the manufacturer's instructions.
Jars should be filled and sealed
while they are still hot.

Contents

Introduction

Modern salads are seriously sexy. Fresh, light and quick to prepare, a salad is how most of us prefer to eat in the warmer months. With more and more people aspiring to eat healthier diets and with such a large variety of fresh vegetables, fruits, grains, seeds and seasonings now available, there has never been a better time to dig out and dust off those salad servers!

This inspiring recipe collection brings together beautifully balanced combinations of ingredients that can be put together in a matter of minutes for time-efficient midweek meals, stylish sharing platters that are fit for entertaining friends and robust salads that will survive being transported and can be enjoyed on the move.

Try a Celeriac Remoulade with Heritage Beetroot & Fennel – an eye-catching dish comprising the wonderful earthy, sweet flavours of beetroot/beets, peppery celeriac, nutty oil and fragrant fennel fronds. Prepare a mouth-watering version of a classic Lebanese mezze, Tomato Fattoush, a vibrant dish of juicy tomatoes, crunchy cucumber and radishes all topped with crisp pitta bread. Or, for a hearty bowl, there's a Wild Rice with Rocket & Pine Nut Salad – not only is this recipe packed with protein, minerals and vitamins it's also a taste and texture sensation.

These salads take their inspiration from countries all around the globe and show just how easy it is to whip up colourful vegetarian and vegan dishes that are full of flavour and texture. From bright and bold Mediterranean recipes to spicy and sweet Asian-inspired classics, from forkfuls of fluffy and fragrant Middle Eastern grains to tangy and spicy Mexican fare, plant-based salads have never been so exciting.

VEGETABLES

Heritage Tomato Fennel Salad

Good, fresh tomatoes need little else to showcase them. Choose the best, varied tomatoes you can find and enjoy them, simply.

15 g/2 tablespoons flaked/slivered almonds

3 tablespoons olive oil

1 tablespoon freshly squeezed lemon juice

1 teaspoon sweet smoked paprika/pimentón

1 large fennel bulb, very thinly sliced (reserve the fronds)

6–8 heritage tomatoes, ideally in assorted varieties, thinly sliced

sea salt and freshly ground black pepper

Serves 4

Toast the flaked/slivered almonds in a small, dry heavy-bottomed frying pan/skillet until golden-brown. Swirl the pan regularly so that they don't burn. Remove from the pan and set aside.

Mix together the oil, lemon juice and smoked paprika/pimentón to make a dressing and season with salt and pepper.

Arrange the fennel and tomato slices on a serving plate. Lightly toss with the dressing, sprinkle over the toasted almonds, garnish with the reserved fennel fronds and serve.

Thai Tomato Salad

This Thai-style salad, with its salty-sweet, chilli/chili-flavoured dressing, is easy to put together. Serve it as a pleasingly textured side dish with a coconut milk-based curry and steamed rice.

16 cherry tomatoes, quartered

200 g/2 cups sugar snap peas, trimmed and halved

1 courgette/zucchini, grated

1 carrot, peeled and grated

2 tablespoons Thai fish sauce

1 tablespoon rice vinegar

2 teaspoons sweet chilli/chili sauce

freshly squeezed juice of ½ lime

50 g/⅓ cup roasted peanuts, finely ground

a handful of fresh Thai basil leaves, to garnish

Serves 4

Toss together the cherry tomatoes, sugar snap peas, courgette/zucchini and carrot in a serving dish.

To make the dressing, mix together the Thai fish sauce, vinegar, sweet chilli/chili sauce and lime juice. Pour over the salad.

Mix in the ground peanuts, garnish with Thai basil leaves and serve at once.

Kachumber

Piquant green chilli/chile, fragrant cumin, tangy lemon juice and fresh mint combine to give a vibrant kick to this classic, easy-to-make, appealingly textured Indian salad.

600 g/1 lb. 5 oz. ripe tomatoes

1 shallot, thinly sliced into semi-circles

1/2 cucumber

2 teaspoons cumin seeds

1 green chilli/chile (such as serrano), deseeded and finely chopped

a handful of fresh mint leaves, shredded

freshly squeezed juice of 1/4 lemon

4 lemon wedges

sea salt and freshly ground black pepper

Serves 4

Begin by scalding the tomatoes. Pour boiling water over the ripe tomatoes in a heatproof bowl. Set aside for 1 minute, then drain and carefully peel off the skins using a sharp knife. Slice the tomatoes in half, scoop out and discard the pulp and slice the tomato shells.

Put the shallot slices into a colander and pour over freshly-boiled water. Pat dry with paper towels and set aside.

Peel the cucumber, slice in half lengthways and scoop out the seeds. Finely slice the flesh and set aside.

Toast the cumin seeds in a small, dry heavy-bottomed frying pan/skillet until fragrant. Swirl the pan regularly so that they don't burn. Remove from the pan and set aside to cool.

Toss together the sliced tomatoes, shallot, cucumber, green chilli/chile and toasted cumin seeds. Season with salt and pepper, add the mint leaves and lemon juice and toss to combine.

Serve at once with a wedge of lemon on the side.

Roast Cauliflower with Almonds & Preserved Lemon

This recipe was born out of a desire to eat quickly, healthily, and of course, tastily.

1 large cauliflower, cut into bite-sized florets

3 tablespoons olive oil

115 g/1 cup whole almonds

1 medium red chilli/chile, deseeded and finely chopped

finely chopped flesh from 1 preserved lemon

a handful of fresh flat-leaf parsley leaves

seeds from 1 whole pomegranate

sea salt and freshly ground black pepper

Serves 4

Preheat the oven to 200°C (400°F) Gas 6.

Put the cauliflower florets on a baking sheet, drizzle over 1 tablespoon of the olive oil and bake in the preheated oven for 30 minutes until the cauliflower is brown and crispy at the edges. Remove from the oven and set aside.

Toast the whole almonds on a separate baking sheet for 6 minutes. Remove from the oven and leave to cool. Coarsely chop and set aside.

Arrange the cauliflower on a platter.

Mix the chilli/chile, remaining olive oil, the chopped preserved lemon and seasoning together in a bowl. Pour the dressing over the cauliflower, then scatter over the parsley, toasted almonds and pomegranate seeds. Serve.

Vegan Caesar Salad

Don't be fooled by the fact that this is a salad – it is a filling meal by itself! Feel free to use different vegetables, but keep the dressing and croutons – this rounds up the salad and makes it delightfully rich.

2 slices bread

1–2 tablespoons olive oil

6–8 leaves of Tuscan kale or young kale

¼ teaspoon sea salt

freshly squeezed juice of 1 lemon

250 g/9 oz. mixed lettuce leaves

½ ripe avocado, cubed

1 medium carrot, finely grated

5 tablespoons alfalfa, garlic, leek, cress or other seed sprouts

4 tablespoons chopped walnuts

10 chive flowers or other edible flowers (optional)

FOR THE MAYONNAISE

300 g/10½ oz. fresh tofu

6 tablespoons water

4 tablespoons olive or sunflower oil

3 tablespoons freshly squeezed lemon juice

1 soft date, stoned/pitted

½ teaspoon sea salt

Serves 2

First make the croutons. Cut the bread into fork-friendly squares and heat the olive oil in a frying pan/skillet. Fry the bread square until golden, then set aside.

Wash and drain the kale leaves and then remove the stem that runs up through the centre of each leaf. Slice the kale thinly, sprinkle with the salt and lemon juice and massage the leaves before letting them marinate for 10 minutes. In a large salad bowl, combine the marinated kale, the lettuce, avocado, carrot, seed sprouts, walnuts, croutons and flowers (if using).

To make the mayonnaise, blend all the ingredients together in a blender until the mixture is completely smooth. Pour over the salad and, with the help of two salad spoons, mix well until completely incorporated. Taste and adjust the seasoning, adding more salt and/or vinegar or spices of choice, if necessary. Leave to rest for 10 minutes before serving, to allow the flavours to develop then serve.

Micro Salad with Parsley Dressing

This salad is inspired by the sorts of vegetables, nuts and seeds that resemble little gems. When combined to make a salad, they create a visually striking effect. Bright colours, a wealth of flavours and a satisfying crunchiness will make every mouthful a delight!

10 baby carrots, scrubbed and thinly sliced

125g/1 cup peas, fresh from their pods

125 g/1 cup raw sweetcorn kernels

80 g/1 cup pomegranate seeds

120 g/1 cup pine nuts

4 tablespoons salt-cured capers

4 tablespoons flaxseed oil

2 tablespoons tamari

2 tablespoons freshly squeezed lemon juice

FOR THE PARSLEY DRESSING

50 g/1 cup fresh parsley leaves, chopped

2 garlic cloves, crushed

4 tablespoons rice vinegar, or other vinegar

60 ml/¼ cup olive oil

grated zest of 1 lemon

4 tablespoons black sesame seeds

sea salt and freshly ground black pepper

Serves 4

Put all the salad ingredients in a salad bowl, mix and allow to stand while you make the parsley dressing.

For the parsley dressing, put all the ingredients except the sesame seeds in a small jar, seal tightly and shake to emulsify the ingredients.

Alternatively, put the ingredients in a small bowl and whisk gently to combine. Add a little water if needed. Season with salt and pepper to taste.

Pour the dressing over the salad and sprinkle the sesame seeds over the top.

Shredded Carrot & Courgette Salad with Sesame Miso Sauce

Vegetables take on a new personality when they are prepared differently. Japanese cuisine can turn a simple radish into a piece of art. The simple act of shredding veggies and mixing in a delicious dressing is a tasty and beautiful way to treat our senses.

2 carrots, grated/shredded

3 courgettes/zucchini, grated

30 g/¼ cup sesame seeds

150 g/1 cup firm tofu, chopped

FOR THE MISO DRESSING

2 tablespoons miso paste

1 tablespoon rice wine vinegar

1 tablespoon sesame oil

2 tablespoons flaxseed oil

1 teaspoon thinly sliced
  fresh ginger

2 teaspoons clear honey

Serves 2-4

Put the carrots, courgettes/zucchini, sesame seeds and tofu in a bowl.

For the dressing, in a small bowl whisk all the ingredients together to an emulsion. Pour over the salad and serve.

The salad can be prepared in advance and stored in an airtight container in the refrigerator for up to 2 days.

Grilled Courgettes with Basil, Mint & Lemon

An elegant side that's perfect for a light lunch or paired with grilled meat. A mandolin slicer is a worthy investment for preparing this salad. It will give you a nasty cut at least once in your life, guaranteed, but you'll heal.

4 courgettes/zucchini, sliced lengthways

olive oil

1 garlic clove, crushed

grated zest and freshly squeezed juice of 1 unwaxed lemon

2–3 sprigs fresh mint leaves, chopped

a small bunch of fresh basil, chopped

a handful of roasted hazelnuts

sea salt and freshly ground black pepper

a ridged grill pan or barbecue

Serves 4

Warm a ridged grill pan or barbecue until it's smoking hot. Brush the courgette/zucchini slices with olive oil and cook on both sides until nicely charred. Remove from the pan or barbecue.

Mix together the crushed garlic, lemon juice, mint, half the basil and a good glug of olive oil. Pour over the grilled courgettes/zucchini. Scatter with the remaining basil, the roasted hazelnuts and lemon zest. Season with salt and pepper and serve.

Raw Parsnip Salad with Curry Dressing

The poor parsnip has been playing second fiddle to the carrot for far too long. It's time to redress the balance. Slice it thinly, avoiding the wooden core, and it can hold its own in any salad.

4 parsnips, peeled

30 g/¼ cup cashew nuts

20 g/2 tablespoons raisins

1 sprig fresh mint, chopped

FOR THE DRESSING

1 white onion, thinly sliced

150 ml/⅔ cup vegetable oil,
   plus extra for frying

1½ tablespoons curry powder

1 egg yolk

1 tablespoon mango chutney

1 teaspoon Dijon mustard

1 teaspoon white wine vinegar

freshly squeezed juice of
   ½ lemon

a small bunch of fresh
   coriander/cilantro,
   finely chopped, plus extra
   to serve

2 tablespoons warm water

sea salt and freshly ground
   black pepper

a food processor

Serves 4-6

First make the dressing. Fry the onion with a little vegetable oil in a frying pan/skillet until it begins to caramelize. Add the curry powder and cook for a further 2 minutes. Remove and allow to cool a little.

Put the onions in the bowl of a food processor. Add a little extra oil to the pan, scrape up the curry powder residue and add to the onions. Add the egg yolk, mango chutney, Dijon mustard and white wine vinegar. Blend to a paste. While blending, add the vegetable oil in a slow, steady stream so it emulsifies to a thick mixture. Add the lemon juice, coriander/cilantro and warm water to loosen. If it's too thick, add a little more water. Season to taste.

Using a vegetable peeler, peel the parsnips into ribbons. Discard the whole core. Mix the parsnips with the cashews and raisins and dress liberally. Scatter with some fresh coriander/cilantro and mint leaves and serve.

Celeriac Remoulade with Heritage Beetroot & Fennel

The balance of the flavours is the key to this dish. The earthy, sweet flavours of the beetroot/beets, the peppery celeriac, the nutty oil and the fragrant fennel fronds combine for melt-in-the-mouth perfection.

8 beetroot/beets of various colours

1 celeriac/celery root

1 teaspoon English mustard

2–3 dashes of Tabasco sauce, or to taste

1 bag of fresh rocket/arugula

fennel fronds, to garnish

sea salt, to season

FOR THE MAYONNAISE

200 ml/³/₄ cup first-press rapeseed oil, plus extra to serve

1 egg

1 teaspoon white wine vinegar

a pinch of table salt

hand-held electric blender and a 300-ml/10-oz. jug/pitcher only slightly larger in diameter than the blade end of the blender

Serves 4

First, make the mayonnaise; add the oil, egg, vinegar and salt to the jug/pitcher and wait for the egg to settle to the bottom. Capture the egg under the base of the blender and, in short bursts of 2–3 seconds, pulse to emulsify the oil and egg together to form mayonnaise. Continue pulsing and slowly draw it up the jug/pitcher until all of the oil is combined to make a thick, yellow mayonnaise.

Preheat the oven to 180°C (350°F) Gas 4.

To prepare the beetroot/beets, heavily salt them and wrap tightly in foil. Place on the middle shelf of the preheated oven and roast for about 45 minutes. Test if they're cooked through by poking with a cocktail stick/toothpick; it should be soft to skewer. Remove from the oven, unwrap from the foil and leave to cool for 30 minutes. Carefully peel off the outer layer, which should fall away easily, leaving you with beautifully cooked beetroot/beets. Slice into thin slices and set aside.

To make the remoulade, peel the celeriac/celery root and carefully chop into matchstick-sized pieces. Mix with the mayonnaise. Add a generous teaspoon of English mustard and a few dashes of Tabasco sauce, to taste.

Assemble a handful of rocket/arugula on each plate. Spoon the remoulade over and arrange the sliced beetroot/beets on top. Drizzle with a little rapeseed oil, garnish with fennel fronds and serve.

Thai Tofu Salad

Hot, sweet and sour are the key flavours of a good dish from Thailand and are all present here.

a small bunch of fresh coriander/cilantro

a bunch of spring onions/scallions, finely chopped

1 stalk fresh lemongrass, finely chopped

2 red bird's eye chillies/chiles, deseeded and finely chopped

2 shallots, finely chopped

50 g/2 oz. fresh galangal (or 30 g/1 oz. fresh ginger), peeled and grated

grated zest of 1 lime

75 g/²⁄₃ cup roasted cashew nuts

50 g/1 cup toasted coconut slices

200 g/3¹⁄₂ cups beansprouts

200 g/1¹⁄₂ cups cubed firm tofu

FOR THE DRESSING

100 ml/¹⁄₃ cup vegetable oil

2 tablespoons sesame oil

seeds of 2 red bird's eye chillies/chiles

2 teaspoons palm sugar/jaggery

freshly squeezed juice of 1 lime

Serves 4

Make the salad dressing by putting all the dressing ingredients in a sealed bottle or jar and shaking vigorously until the sugar/jaggery is dissolved. Set aside.

Finely chop the coriander/cilantro stalks, setting the leaves aside. Toss with the spring onions/scallions, lemongrass, chillies/chiles and shallots in a large mixing bowl.

Add the galangal or ginger, then add the lime zest, half the cashews and the toasted coconut slices.

To serve, divide half the beansprouts between four plates. Arrange the tofu on top. Mix the remaining beansprouts with the other salad ingredients and pile on top of the tofu. Dress generously with the salad dressing and finish with a sprinkle of coriander/cilantro leaves and the remaining cashew nuts.

Summer Vegetable Carpaccio

In this refreshing carpaccio, the nearly transparent slices of vegetable are enhanced with a tangy sour-sweet Asian dressing. You can use any firm vegetable you have in your fridge – the key is to slice them paper-thin so that they can absorb the dressing and tenderize. It makes a lovely light appetizer or side dish.

5 large radishes

1/2 fennel bulb

1 large courgette/zucchini

1/2 red onion

FOR THE ASIAN DRESSING

1 garlic clove, crushed

2 teaspoons finely chopped (peeled) fresh ginger

1 tomato, skinned and finely chopped

1 tablespoon freshly chopped mint

1 tablespoon freshly chopped coriander/cilantro

grated zest of 1 lime and freshly squeezed juice of 1/2 lime

3 tablespoons extra virgin olive oil

1/2 tablespoon rice wine or white wine vinegar

1/2 red chilli/chile, deseeded and finely chopped

1 1/2 teaspoons granulated sugar

sea salt and freshly ground black pepper

Serves 4-6

Using a mandoline, vegetable peeler or very sharp knife, carefully slice the radishes, fennel, courgette/zucchini and red onion as thinly as possibly. Put the prepared vegetables in a bowl, cover and set aside while you make the Asian dressing.

To make the Asian dressing, simply put all the ingredients in a small bowl and whisk with a fork until well combined.

To assemble, pour the dressing over the prepared vegetables and toss well to coat evenly. Use salad servers to arrange the salad on serving plates and serve immediately.

Asian-style Hot & Sour Salad with Marinated Tofu

100 g/about 1 cup asparagus tips

100 g/about 1 cup mangetout/snow peas

50 g/¹/₃ cup toasted cashews

100 g/2 cups beansprouts

100 g/3¹/₂ oz. rice noodles (optional)

1 carrot, sliced into ribbons

1 tablespoon toasted sesame seeds, to serve

FOR THE MARINATED TOFU

2 tablespoons sesame oil

1 tablespoon dark soy sauce or tamari

¹/₂ red chilli/chile, finely chopped

1 teaspoon grated (peeled) fresh ginger

grated zest and freshly squeezed juice of ¹/₂ lime

¹/₂ teaspoon sugar

200 g/7 oz. tofu

FOR THE DRESSING

¹/₂ teaspoon sea salt

2 teaspoons sugar

grated zest and freshly squeezed juice of 1 lime

1 teaspoon white wine vinegar

¹/₂ red chilli/chile

Serves 4

This crunchy salad is perfect for a light lunch or as a small dish to serve as part of an Asian meal. You can use any fresh vegetables that you have to hand.

For the marinated tofu, put all the ingredients except the tofu in a bowl and stir until well combined. Put the tofu in a separate bowl, pour the marinade over it and set aside to marinate for 30 minutes.

Bring a saucepan of water to the boil and cook the asparagus and mangetout/snow peas for 3 minutes, until they soften slightly but still have a crunch to them. Remove them from the boiling water and put them into a bowl of ice-cold water to stop the cooking process. Drain, then slice in half lengthways and put them in a serving bowl. Add the cashews to the serving bowl.

If you are using rice noodles, cook them according to the packet instructions, then drain.

Put all the dressing ingredients in a bowl and stir until well combined. Add the rest of the salad ingredients to the serving bowl, add the dressing and toss to coat the salad. Crumble the marinated tofu over the salad and finish with a sprinkling of sesame seeds. Serve.

Tomato Fattoush

Crisp pitta bread contrasted with juicy tomatoes and crunchy cucumber and radishes makes this version of a classic Lebanese mezze dish a salad to relish.

1 pitta bread

2½ tablespoons extra virgin olive oil

500 g/1 lb. tomatoes, thickly sliced

½ cucumber, halved lengthways and sliced

6 radishes, thinly sliced

1 spring onion/scallion, finely chopped

freshly squeezed juice of ½ lemon

a pinch of sea salt

2 tablespoons freshly chopped flat-leaf parsley

2 teaspoons ground sumac

Serves 4

Slice the pitta around its edges to form two thin pitta halves. Brush with ½ tablespoon of the olive oil and grill/broil under a medium heat for 2–3 minutes until golden-brown and crisp. Cool, then tear into small pieces.

Toss together the tomatoes, cucumber, radishes and spring onion/scallion in a serving bowl.

To make the dressing, mix together the remaining olive oil and the lemon juice, season with the salt and pour over the salad. Mix in the crisp pitta bread pieces and parsley.

Sprinkle with the sumac and serve at once.

FRUIT, NUTS & SEEDS

Peach Panzanella

Tuscans beware, this isn't a classic panzanella. The mellow sweetness of the grilled peaches works perfectly with the crunchy bread and olive oil. You can add rocket/arugula or other leaves if you want more greens.

1/2 small red onion, very thinly sliced

1/2 tablespoon red wine vinegar

2 peaches, stoned/pitted and cut into 2-cm/3/4-in. wedges

2 tablespoons olive oil, plus extra for brushing and drizzling

15 baby plum tomatoes, halved

1 avocado, peeled, stoned/pitted and cut into bite-sized chunks

1 full-length slice of sourdough bread

1 small garlic clove, halved

a bunch of fresh basil, roughly chopped

1 teaspoon Thai red chilli/chili paste

sea salt and freshly ground black pepper

Serves 2

Place the sliced red onion in a bowl with the red wine vinegar and a pinch of sea salt. Toss together and set aside to allow the flavours to infuse.

Place a grill pan over a high heat. Lightly brush the peach wedges with just enough olive oil to coat them. Add the peaches to the pan and cook for a couple of minutes until charred on one side. Flip over and cook on the other side. Transfer to a plate while you prepare the other ingredients.

In a large mixing bowl gently toss the chopped tomatoes and avocado chunks together with the cooked peaches in 1 tablespoon of the olive oil and a good pinch of salt. Set aside.

Toast the sliced sourdough bread until golden brown and crunchy on the outside. Rub the garlic clove on the hot bread, then drizzle some olive oil over the bread and leave it to soak in.

Finely chop the leftover garlic and add it to the tomato mix, together with the chopped basil and vinegar-infused red onion slices.

For the dressing, combine the Thai red chilli/chili paste with the remaining tablespoon of olive oil in a small bowl. Add this into the salad bowl and then tear the bread into the salad in rough chunks. Gently combine everything together until well mixed. Taste and season with black pepper and more sea salt if needed. Serve.

Lemon, Fennel & Rocket Salad with Radicchio

This refreshingly light salad is bursting with flavours brought to life by the sweet, bright zing of lemon.

- ½ radicchio (red chicory), the leaves torn into large shreds
- 2 large lemons, peeled and thinly sliced
- 1 fennel bulb, peeled and thinly sliced
- a generous handful of rocket/arugula, torn if the leaves are large

FOR THE DRESSING
- 2 tablespoons olive oil
- 2 tablespoons finely grated Parmesan cheese
- a few drops of balsamic vinegar
- sea salt and freshly ground black pepper

Serves 4

Arrange the radicchio on four individual plates. Add the lemon slices, fennel and rocket/arugula.

To make the dressing, mix together the olive oil, Parmesan cheese and vinegar in a small bowl and season to taste with salt and pepper.

Pour the dressing over the plated salad just before serving.

Rocket, Black Olive, Feta & Orange Salad

Hot rocket/arugula leaves bring this Mediterranean-style salad alive, making it perfect for summer dining. Always buy the best extra virgin olive oil and olives you can find.

100 g/³/4 cup cubed feta cheese

2 oranges

2 sprigs fresh thyme

60 g/generous 1 cup rocket/arugula

1 red onion, thinly sliced into rings

a handful of toasted flaked/slivered almonds

100 g/1 cup stoned/pitted black olives

olive oil, to drizzle

sea salt

Serves 4

Crumble the feta cheese into a large mixing bowl.

Zest the oranges and set aside. Cut the peel and pith from the oranges, then slice the segments out by using a small, sharp knife between the membranes and add to the bowl.

Pick the thyme leaves from the stalks and add to the bowl.

Add the remaining ingredients except the olive oil and salt and toss to fully combine.

Drizzle with ample olive oil and sprinkle with a good pinch of sea salt before serving.

Watermelon, Black Olive & Rose Water Salad

It is not perhaps the most obvious choice of ingredients for a salad, but when you think about it, salty olives and sweet watermelon are the perfect pairing, playing off each other beautifully.

600 g/1¼ lb. watermelon, seeds and skin removed

2 teaspoons rose water

½ red onion, thinly sliced

small handful of fresh flat-leaf parsley and mint leaves, chopped, plus extra to garnish

100 g/²/₃ cup black olives, stoned/pitted

Serves 4

Cut the watermelon into bite-sized chunks and toss gently with the rose water in a bowl. Add in the red onion, flat-leaf parsley and mint and black olives and mix together.

Keep refrigerated until ready to serve. Sprinkle over the remaining herbs to garnish.

Camargue Red Rice Salad with Black Grapes, Pecans & Marjoram

Camargue red rice from southern France is a short-grain, slightly chewy rice, not dissimilar to the sticky short-grain rice of South-east Asia, or brown rice from Korea and Japan. In a salad like this it is wonderful, not just a carby mass to accompany the other ingredients, but as a stand-out flavour and texture all of its own. If you are looking for a substitute, go for a short-grain Asian brown rice or farro.

80 g/^{1}/$_2$ cup pecan nuts

400 g/2 cups Camargue red rice

2^1/$_2$ tablespoons good-quality balsamic vinegar

1 small garlic clove, crushed

2 teaspoons pure maple syrup

zest of 1 lemon

3 tablespoons extra virgin olive oil

^{1}/$_2$ red onion, halved and very thinly sliced

150 g/5 oz. black grapes

a handful of marjoram leaves, or oregano or basil

small handful of rocket/arugula

sea salt and freshly ground black pepper

Serves 4-6

Preheat the oven to 180°C (350°F) Gas 4.

Place the pecan nuts in a roasting pan and roast the nuts in the preheated oven for 3–4 minutes, until they're a shade darker and aromatic. Remove from the oven and set aside.

Bring a large saucepan of salted water to the boil, add in the rice and simmer for 20–25 minutes until cooked. It should still be a bit chewy. Strain off the water completely and leave the rice to dry out in the warm saucepan.

In a bowl, combine the vinegar, garlic, maple syrup, lemon zest and olive oil. Season to taste with salt and pepper and then, when the rice has dried out but is still warm, pour over and combine. Add in the red onion, reserved pecans and the grapes and gently mix together. When you are ready to serve, mix in the marjoram. Taste and adjust the seasoning if necessary, then sprinkle a few rocket/arugula leaves over the top, before tumbling onto a large serving dish. Serve at room temperature.

Spicy & Sweet Salad with Kumquats & Brazil Nuts

Kumquats are a small, oval fruit with a strong and pleasant citrus smell. They grow on the coast and can be eaten whole, without peeling. They have a sweet rind that contrasts with the juicy, sour centre and are a wonderful addition to salads.

150 g/3²/₃ cups wild rocket/ arugula

150 g/3 cups curly endive

10–15 kumquats (or seedless mandarin segments if you can't find kumquats)

60 g/¹/₂ cup Brazil nuts, chopped

FOR THE DRESSING

2 tablespoons raw clear honey or agave nectar

1 tablespoon chilli/chile-infused olive oil

2 tablespoons chia seed oil, or other oil

4 tablespoons freshly squeezed lemon juice

sea salt and freshly ground black pepper

Serves 4

Wash the rocket/arugula, endive and kumquats well. Cut the kumquats into thin slices.

For the dressing, put the honey or agave nectar, olive oil, chia seed oil and lemon juice in a small jar, seal tightly and shake to emulsify the ingredients. Alternatively, put the ingredients in a small bowl and whisk gently to combine. Add a little water if needed. Season with salt and pepper to taste.

Put the greens, kumquats and Brazil nuts in a salad bowl and add the dressing. Mix gently, then serve immediately before the greens have time to wilt.

The Brazil nuts are interchangeable with any other nuts you have in the cupboard.

Avocado, Rocket & Grapefruit Salad with Sunflower Seeds

This recipe is elegant, simple and classic. The addition of sunflower seeds and flaxseed/linseed oil boost the omega-3 content. And any size or shape plate will work fine!

2 pink grapefruits

2 medium ripe avocados

100 g/4 cups rocket/arugula

FOR THE VINAIGRETTE

1 teaspoon clear honey

3 tablespoons champagne vinegar

4 tablespoons flaxseed/linseed oil

3 tablespoons sunflower seeds

sea salt and freshly ground black pepper

Serves 4

Prepare the grapefruits. Peel each fruit whole, then break into individual segments. Using a sharp knife, carefully score the straight edge of each segment, then peel the membrane from the flesh. Repeat until you have released all the deliciously juicy segments. Halve, stone/pit, peel and slice the avocados.

For the vinaigrette, whisk the honey, champagne vinegar and flaxseed/linseed oil together in a mixing bowl, adding the sunflower seeds at the last minute so as not to damage them. Season to taste.

Place a layer of rocket/arugula on each plate. Arrange the grapefruit and avocado on top, with alternating slices of grapefruit and avocado in concentric semi-circles. You needn't arrange the fruit in this way if you're in a hurry, but it looks great when entertaining. Lightly drizzle a line of vinaigrette horizontally across the half-moons of alternating grapefruit and avocado. Enjoy immediately.

Wild Rice with Artichokes, Peaches & Pine Nuts

1 litre/4 cups water

190 g/1 cup wild rice

400 g/1½ cups artichokes
soaked in water
(rinsed and drained)

a bunch of freshly chopped
coriander/cilantro

30 g/¼ cup pine nuts

60 g/½ cup chopped peaches

FOR THE DRESSING

3 tablespoons walnut oil

2 tablespoons freshly squeezed
lemon juice

½ teaspoon sea salt

½ teaspoon freshly ground
black pepper

Serves 2–4

Wild rice is actually an edible grass, which has a slightly nutty and chewy flavour. It forms the base of a great grain salad – just add your favourite veggies and a simple vinaigrette.

Bring the water to the boil in a large saucepan or pot over a high heat. Add the wild rice, reduce the heat, cover and simmer for 45 minutes until tender. Drain any excess water and set aside.

For the dressing, whisk together the walnut oil, lemon juice, salt and pepper in a large bowl.

Once the rice has cooled a bit but is still slightly warm, mix in the dressing with the artichokes, half of the coriander/cilantro, the pine nuts and peaches.

Serve with an extra garnish of the remaining coriander/cilantro.

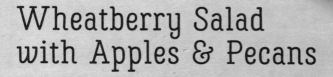

Wheatberry Salad with Apples & Pecans

This is a wholegrain version of a Waldorf salad.
If you're looking for a gluten-free version, buckwheat
is a great substitute for the wheatberries here.

200 g/1 cup wheatberries

1 green apple, cored and chopped

65 g/¹⁄₂ cup pecan halves

100 g/2 cups mixed salad leaves

FOR THE DRESSING

50 g/scant ¹⁄₄ cup mayonnaise

50 g/scant ¹⁄₄ cup low-fat yogurt

3 tablespoons freshly squeezed lemon juice

¹⁄₂ teaspoon sea salt

¹⁄₂ teaspoon freshly ground black pepper

Serves 2–4

Put the wheatberries in a medium-sized saucepan
or pot and cover completely with water by 2.5 cm/1 inch.

Bring to the boil over a high heat, then reduce the heat and
simmer, uncovered, for about 50 minutes. Remove from the
heat, drain and set aside.

In a large bowl, make the dressing by whisking together
the mayonnaise, yogurt, lemon juice, salt and pepper. Add
the apple, pecans and wheatberries, and using salad tongs
or a large spoon, gently fold all the ingredients together.

Plate the salad leaves first, then add the wheatberry mix
on top. Serve immediately as the apple will soon discolour.

Crunchy Fennel Salad with Pomegranate, Mango & Walnuts

Fennel is ubiquitous nowadays, as it rightfully should be. This is a great salad by itself, or as an accompaniment to grilled fish. Don't be scared to use the whole of the fennel – it adds colour to the dish. Reserve some of the sprightly leaves for decoration.

olive oil, for frying

50 g/½ cup walnut halves

1 pomegranate

2 large or 4 small fennel bulbs, halved lengthways and thinly sliced

1 small red onion, thinly sliced

1 firm mango, stoned/pitted, peeld and thinly sliced

1 red chilli/chile, thinly sliced

1 tablespoon freshly chopped coriander/cilantro

1 teaspoon fresh lemon thyme leaves

freshly squeezed juice of 1 lime

sea salt and freshly ground black pepper

Serves 4

Heat a splash of olive oil in a non-stick frying pan/skillet, add the walnuts and toast gently until golden brown. Once they're just right, remove from the pan and set aside. (If you leave them in, the residual heat will keep toasting them and before you know it you'll have blackened, bitter nuts.)

Remove the pomegranate seeds by cutting the fruit in half, holding it over a bowl and bashing the outside with the back of a wooden spoon so that the seeds fall into the bowl.

Mix all the ingredients together, season with salt and pepper and serve.

Red Cabbage, Beetroot, Feta & Apricot Salad

This is a vibrant, colourful salad that marries the sweetness of ripe apricots with the saltiness of feta.

4 beetroot/beets, peeled

1 small red cabbage

3 spring onions/scallions

150 g/5 oz. fresh apricots, stoned/pitted and sliced

a small bunch of fresh flat-leaf parsley, roughly chopped

150 g/5 oz. feta cheese

olive oil, for dressing

sea salt and freshly ground black pepper

a food processor with slicing and grating attachments

Serves 6–8

Grate the beetroot/beets in the food processor using the medium grating attachment, then slice the red cabbage and spring onions/scallions using the thin slicing attachment.

Mix all the ingredients together except the feta and olive oil. Season gently (remembering that feta is quite salty) and crumble the feta on top. Drizzle over the olive oil and serve.

Pimm's Salad

Pimm's No. 1 Cup is traditionally served with mint, cucumber and a medley of chopped fresh summer fruits. This is a take on the classic drink, using the cocktail garnishes as a base for a quick and fun summery salad, perfect for al fresco lunches.

150 g/1½ cups strawberries, hulled and thinly sliced

1 large cucumber, peeled

a small bunch of fresh mint

grated zest and freshly squeezed juice of 1 lemon

50 g/1 cup fresh rocket/arugula

50 g/1 cup fresh watercress

150 ml/⅔ cup olive oil

1½ tablespoons white wine vinegar

50 ml/3½ tablespoons Pimm's No. 1 cup or other summer gin cup

1 lemon, cut into 4 wedges

Serves 4

Put the strawberries in a large mixing bowl and set aside.

Using a peeler, make long ribbons of the cucumber and add to the bowl with the strawberries. Discard the seedy centre of the cucumber.

Pick two-thirds of the mint leaves and crush them a little before adding to the bowl; save the remaining leaves to dress the salad. Add the lemon zest, rocket/arugula and watercress to the bowl. Toss the leaves together to combine.

To make a vinaigrette, pour the lemon juice, olive oil, white wine vinegar and Pimm's into a jar with a screw-top lid. Tighten the lid and shake well to combine.

Pour about one-quarter of the vinaigrette down the side of the bowl with the salad ingredients and turn the salad over several times to coat.

To serve, arrange the salad on four plates and dress with the remaining mint leaves and a lemon wedge. Pour the remaining vinaigrette into a jug/pitcher and bring to the table with a serving spoon.

GRAINS

Tomato, Freekeh & Avocado Salad

Freekeh's slightly chewy texture and nutty flavour contrasts nicely with the tomato and avocado in this simple, Middle Eastern-inspired salad. Serve as part of a buffet meal or as a side dish.

100 g/²/₃ cup freekeh

1 ripe avocado, peeled, stoned/pitted and diced

freshly squeezed juice of ¹/₂ lemon

12 cherry tomatoes, quartered

2 sun-dried tomatoes in oil, drained and chopped

1 spring onion/scallion, finely chopped

2 tablespoons argan oil (or walnut oil)

2 tablespoons freshly chopped parsley

1 tablespoon pine nuts, toasted

sea salt

Serves 4

Cook the freekeh in a pan of boiling, salted water, simmering it for 15–20 minutes until tender. Drain and allow to cool.

Toss the avocado with a little of the lemon juice to prevent any discolouration.

Mix together the cooked freekeh, cherry tomatoes, sun-dried tomatoes and spring onion/scallion. Toss with the oil, the remaining lemon juice and parsley. Fold in the diced avocado, top with the pine nuts and serve at once.

Tomato Tabbouleh

This zingy tomato and parsley salad is a Lebanese classic, traditionally served as a mezze dish.

1 tablespoon bulgur wheat

350 g/12 oz. ripe but firm tomatoes

100 g/1 cup fresh flat-leaf parsley

1 spring onion/scallion, finely chopped

2 tablespoons thinly sliced fresh mint leaves

freshly squeezed juice of 1 lemon

2 tablespoons extra virgin olive oil

sea salt and freshly ground black pepper

fresh mint sprigs, to garnish

Serves 4

Soak the bulgur wheat in cold water for 15 minutes to soften.

Meanwhile, finely dice the tomatoes, discarding the white stem core. Trim off and discard the stalks of the flat-leaf parsley and finely chop the leaves. If using a food processor, take care not to over-chop the parsley as it may turn to a pulp; you want the parsley to retain its texture.

Drain the soaked bulgur wheat, squeezing it dry of excess moisture. Toss together the diced tomatoes, chopped parsley, bulgur wheat, spring onion/scallion and mint. Add the lemon juice and olive oil, season with salt and pepper, and toss well.

Garnish the tabbouleh with mint sprigs and serve at once.

Hazelnut, Mushroom & Bulgur Wheat Salad

Thinly sliced mushrooms are a great addition to salads, adding a fresh, clean flavour and distinctive, delicate texture. Here they are combined to good effect with dry-fried hazelnuts, juicy tomatoes, bulgur wheat and a tangy pomegranate molasses dressing to make a vibrant, colourful salad, inspired by the flavours of the Middle East.

100 g/1/2 cup bulgur wheat

100 g/2/3 cup blanched
   hazelnuts

100 g/3/4 cup cherry tomatoes,
   quartered

1/2 red (bell) pepper,
   deseeded and diced

1 spring onion/scallion,
   finely chopped

3 tablespoons extra virgin
   olive oil

3 tablespoons pomegranate
   molasses

50 g/1 small bunch fresh
   parsley, very finely chopped

150 g/51/2 oz. white/cup
   mushrooms, thinly sliced

sea salt and freshly ground
   black pepper

Serves 4

Soak the bulgur wheat in boiling water for 5 minutes to soften; drain.

Dry-fry the hazelnuts in a frying pan/skillet for 2–3 minutes until golden-brown, stirring often. Leave to cool and then finely chop.

In a large bowl, mix together the bulgur wheat, toasted hazelnuts, cherry tomatoes, red (bell) pepper and spring onion/scallion. Add the olive oil and pomegranate molasses. Season well with salt and black pepper, and mix thoroughly. Mix in the parsley, then the mushrooms. Serve at once.

Lemon Summer Grain Salad

2 courgettes/zucchini,
  thinly sliced lengthways

mild olive oil, for brushing

1 tablespoon za'atar

155 g/1 cup fresh podded peas

2 x 250 g/8 oz. pouches
  ready-cooked grains
  (such as a mixture of barley,
  wheatberries, spelt and rice)

a handful of fresh mint leaves

3 handfuls of pea shoots

FOR THE DRESSING

grated zest and freshly
  squeezed juice of 2 lemons

1 tablespoon harissa paste

3 tablespoons olive oil

Serves 4

Pouches of ready-cooked grains are so convenient. You could cook your own selection of grains if you wish, but this makes the preparation more time-consuming.

Heat a griddle or barbecue until hot. Brush the courgettes/zucchini with olive oil, sprinkle over the za'atar and cook in batches for 2 minutes on each side until tender and seared. Remove from the heat and set aside. Tip the peas into a pan of boiling water, cook for 3 minutes, then drain and set aside.

Tip the pouches of grains into a large bowl and break up with a fork.

For the dressing, whisk together the lemon zest and juice, harissa and olive oil. Add to the grains and toss to coat evenly.

Gently combine the courgettes/zucchini, peas, mint leaves and pea shoots with the dressed grains. Serve immediately.

Grilled Lettuce & Spelt Lemon Salad

This salad is a stand-alone salad but could be served as a side dish if you prefer. The crunchy lettuce and croutons are immensely satisfying.

75 g/½ cup spelt

2 slices of sourdough bread

3 tablespoons olive oil

2 Little Gem or Romaine
  lettuces, quartered

a generous handful of
  fresh tarragon leaves

a handful of fresh flat-leaf
  parsley, roughly chopped

50 g/⅔ cup Parmigiano
  Reggiano, shaved

FOR THE DRESSING

grated zest and segments
  of 1 unwaxed lemon

1 teaspoon clear honey

2 teaspoons pernod

1 small preserved lemon,
  halved, deseeded and
  thinly sliced

1 garlic clove, crushed

1 small shallot, finely chopped

2 tablespoons olive oil

sea salt and freshly ground
  black pepper

Serves 4

Preheat the oven to 220°C (425°F) Gas 7.

Bring a small pan of water to the boil, add the spelt and cook according to the pack instructions. Drain, refresh and set aside.

For the dressing, add the lemon zest and segments to a bowl along with the honey, pernod, preserved lemon, garlic, shallot and olive oil, plus a little salt and pepper. Mix well.

Drizzle the bread with 2 tablespoons of the olive oil, place on a baking sheet and bake in the preheated oven for 6–8 minutes until golden. Turn the bread over and bake for a further 3–4 minutes.

Heat a griddle pan until hot, brush the lettuce quarters with the remaining olive oil and griddle until lightly coloured on the outside.

Place the lettuce quarters on a serving platter. Tear the toasted bread into small pieces and scatter over the lettuce quarters along with the spelt and the lemon dressing. Garnish with the tarragon, parsley and Parmigiano Reggiano shavings and serve.

Quinoa with Mint, Orange & Beetroot

The orange cuts through the earthy flavour of the beetroot/beets and keeps the quinoa nice and moist.

4 beetroot/beets (about 400 g/14 oz.), scrubbed clean

2 teaspoons olive oil

1 tablespoon good-quality balsamic vinegar

300 g/1½ cups quinoa

1 teaspoon fennel seeds

1 teaspoon cumin seeds

2 oranges, one zested

a large handful of fresh mint leaves, chopped, plus extra for serving

a small handful of fresh flat-leaf parsley leaves, chopped

grated zest of 1 lemon

olive oil, for dressing

sea salt and freshly ground black pepper

Serves 4-6

Preheat the oven to 200°C (400°F) Gas 6.

Trim the beetroot/beet stalks, but leave about 2.5 cm/1 inch on the top. Cut the beetroot/beets into 2-cm/¾-inch thick wedges, toss in the olive oil and season with salt and pepper. Place in a roasting pan and roast for 30–40 minutes until blistered and a sharp knife slides into the flesh with ease. Remove and toss with the balsamic vinegar while still hot.

Bring the quinoa to the boil in just under double its quantity of salted water. The moment it comes to the boil, reduce the heat to low and place the lid on top. Cook for about 12 minutes until all the water has been absorbed. Turn off the heat, remove the lid and let any remaining water evaporate. Remove to a wide plate or tray and leave to cool.

Place the fennel and cumin seeds in a dry frying pan/skillet over a medium heat for a few minutes until aromatic. Turn the heat off.

Grate the zest of one orange and set aside. Then, cut the top and bottom off both oranges, just down to the flesh, then place the oranges on their ends, cut-side down, and carefully, following the shape of the orange, cut the skin off in strips from top to bottom, removing all the pith. Segment the oranges by cutting the flesh away from the membrane. Reserve the juice that has come out during preparation.

In a large bowl, combine the quinoa with the chopped herbs, seeds, orange zest and lemon zest and season to taste with salt and pepper. Add in most of the beetroot/beets and orange segments (and reserved juice) and a little extra virgin olive oil. Combine and serve at room temperature with the remaining beetroot/beets and orange segments on top and a few fresh mint leaves sprinkled over.

Wild Rice with Rocket & Pine Nuts

Wild rice has a wonderful taste and texture – it's a type of grass native to the Great Lakes region of North America. High in protein, fibre, minerals and vitamins, wild rice should have its place in your weekly menu. And when mixed as below, it'll be delicious, too!

250 ml/1 cup water

110 g/²/3 cup wild rice

a pinch of sea salt

60 g/¹/2 cup black olives, stoned/pitted and chopped

70 g/¹/2 cup lightly toasted pine nuts or other nuts/seeds

4 handfuls of rocket/arugula, baby spinach or any other soft greens

FOR THE MEDITERRANEAN VINAIGRETTE

60 ml/¹/4 cup olive oil

balsamic or apple cider vinegar, to taste

a handful of fresh basil leaves, finely chopped

1 garlic clove, crushed

4 tablespoons water

sea salt and freshly ground black pepper

Serves 1-2

In a saucepan, bring the water to the boil and add the rice and salt, then reduce the heat, cover and cook for about 45 minutes or until the rice is soft and the water is completely absorbed. (If wild rice isn't available, then you can use any other non-sticky cooked whole grains and add them to the olives and pine nuts.)

For the vinaigrette, place all the ingredients in a jar, close and shake. In a large salad bowl, mix together the cooked rice, olives and pine nuts. Add the vinaigrette and mix well. Rinse and drain the greens, then add to the salad just before serving.

Pink Quinoa Salad with Fennel & Arame

Having a plate full of lively colours every day of the week keeps you healthy inside out! The beetroot/beet brings an amazingly vibrant pink colour to this salad!

170 g/1 cup quinoa

130 g/1¹⁄₃ cups thinly sliced fennel bulb

3 tablespoons freshly squeezed lemon juice

20 g/1 cup dried arame strips

1 teaspoon tamari

¹⁄₂ small beetroot/beet, peeled and finely grated

1 tablespoon umeboshi vinegar

3 tablespoons sesame oil

3 spring onions/scallions, finely chopped

2 tablespoons dry-roasted sunflower seeds (optional)

sea salt

Serves 2

In a saucepan, bring 400 ml/1³⁄₄ cups of the water to the boil.

Wash the quinoa, drain it well and add it to the boiling water together with ¹⁄₄ teaspoon salt. Reduce the heat, cover and simmer for 20 minutes or until the water is completely absorbed and then turn off the heat.

Place the sliced fennel in a bowl, add 2 tablespoons of the lemon juice and ¹⁄₂ teaspoon salt and squeeze well with your hands, until the fennel starts 'sweating'.

To cook the arame, put the strips in a small saucepan, add the remaining water and bring to the boil, uncovered. Reduce the heat, half-cover and cook for 15 minutes. Drain off the excess water, add the tamari and quickly stir over a low heat until it is absorbed.

In a large salad bowl, mix the grated beetroot/beet with the vinegar, which helps to accentuate the bright pink colour. Add the cooked quinoa, the remaining lemon juice, 4 tablespoons of the cooked arame and the sesame oil. Just before serving, mix in the fennel and spring onions/scallions. Taste and season with some more salt and lemon juice, if necessary. To add extra texture to this salad, sprinkle the dry-roasted sunflower seeds over it. Serve.

Pearled Spelt Salad with Button Mushrooms & Watercress

Spelt has a nice chewy texture, both whole grain and pearled. Using pearled is less time-consuming, as it cooks in 20 minutes. Combined with a refreshing dressing, it makes for a light and nutritious lunch.

440 ml/scant 2 cups water

190 g/1 cup pearled spelt, washed and drained

¼ teaspoon sea salt

150 g/2 cups sliced button mushrooms

3 teaspoons tamari

1 teaspoon freshly squeezed lemon juice

1 teaspoon sesame oil

3 tablespoons chopped dry-roasted hazelnuts, to garnish

FOR THE DRESSING

2 handfuls of watercress, washed and drained

¼ teaspoon sea salt, or to taste

2 tablespoons chopped hazelnuts

2 tablespoons olive oil

2 tablespoons freshly squeezed lemon juice

Serves 2

In a saucepan, bring the water to the boil, then add the spelt and salt, reduce the heat to a minimum and cover. Cook for 20 minutes or until the spelt is chewy but soft. Drain any liquid that remains, if any, and allow the spelt to cool slightly.

Coat the mushrooms in the tamari and lemon juice. Heat the sesame oil in a heavy-bottomed frying pan/skillet, then add the mushrooms and fry for only 1–2 minutes until the mushrooms start wilting slightly. Turn off the heat, transfer the mushrooms to a bowl and leave to cool.

To prepare the green dressing, place all the ingredients, except a couple or so watercress sprigs to garnish the dish at the end, in a blender jug and blend until smooth and creamy. Taste and adjust the seasoning, if necessary. The dressing should be slightly salty to enhance the flavour of the cooked spelt.

When you are ready to serve, combine the spelt and mushrooms and top with 2 generous tablespoons of the dressing. Sprinkle with the chopped hazelnuts and add the reserved watercress sprigs. Let each person mix in the dressing just before eating.

Quinoa Salad with Spring Vegetables & Herbs in a Citrus Dressing

315 g/1½ cups quinoa

360 ml/scant 1½ cups
  vegetable stock

300 ml/1¼ cups water

1 avocado, peeled, stoned/
  pitted and cut into bite-sized
  pieces

40 g/¼ cup segmented
  clementines, cut into
  bite-sized pieces

45 g/⅓ cup thinly sliced
  radishes

70 g/⅔ cup watercress,
  plus extra to serve

45 g/¼ cup pomegranate seeds

40 g/¼ cup pine nuts

8 g/⅛ cup fresh basil leaves

15 g/¼ cup freshly chopped
  flat-leaf parsley

CITRUS DRESSING

6 tablespoons flaxseed/linseed
  oil

2 tablespoons freshly squeezed
  lemon juice

freshly squeezed juice
  of 2 clementines

1 teaspoon clear honey

1 teaspoon Dijon mustard

sea salt and freshly ground
  black pepper

Serves 4-6

If you want to convert a friend to the wonders of quinoa, try serving this for lunch. There is nothing as enticing as a gorgeous quinoa salad, which looks almost too pretty to eat.

Put the quinoa in a large saucepan or pot with the vegetable stock and water over a medium-high heat. Bring to the boil, then reduce the heat, cover and simmer for 20 minutes. Remove from the heat, fluff with a fork, cover once more and let it sit for another 5 minutes. Remove the lid and set aside to cool.

Prepare the remaining salad ingredients. Mix the avocado, clementines and radishes together in a bowl with the watercress, pomegranate seeds and pine nuts. Gently roll and finely chop the basil and flat-leaf parsley, then add to the mix.

For the dressing, whisk together the flaxseed oil, lemon and clementine juices, honey and Dijon mustard. Season with salt and pepper to taste.

Mix the quinoa with the bowl of salad and drizzle some of the dressing on top.

Serve on individual plates with extra watercress and dressing to the side, if desired.

Shaved Broccoli & Buckwheat Salad with Dukkah Topping

This salad uses the forgotten broccoli stems that can be quite attractive shaved into strips. Dukkah is a special addition to any salad. It is made from crushed seeds, nuts and spices that are tasty and great for digestion, which is a win-win!

250 ml/1 cup vegetable stock

250 ml/1 cup water

185 g/1 cup buckwheat groats

4 broccoli stalks

15 g/1/8 cup chopped hazelnuts

FOR THE DRESSING

300 g/1 cup natural yogurt

freshly squeezed juice
  of 2 lemons

1/2 teaspoon sea salt

1/2 teaspoon ground cumin

a bunch of freshly chopped
  coriander/cilantro

FOR THE DUKKAH TOPPING

2 teaspoons cumin seeds

2 teaspoons coriander seeds

1 teaspoon fennel seeds

100 g/3/4 cup roasted hazelnuts,
  chopped

100 g/3/4 cup roasted sunflower
  seeds

1 teaspoon sea salt

Serves 4-6

In a large saucepan or pot, put the vegetable stock, water and buckwheat groats over a medium-high heat. Bring to the boil, then reduce the heat and simmer for 15 minutes with the lid half on, stirring once halfway through. Be careful not to overcook the groats. Drain and rinse with cold water then set aside in a bowl to cool.

Peel and shave the broccoli stalks into ribbons using a vegetable peeler or mandolin, then add to a large saucepan or pot of boiling water. Cook for 3 minutes, drain, then refresh the broccoli to suspend the cooking by submerging it in a bowl of iced water. Drain, cool and mix with the hazelnuts and cooled buckwheat.

For the dressing, whisk all the ingredients together, cover and store in the refrigerator until you are ready to serve.

For the dukkah topping, use a pestle and mortar to grind the cumin, coriander and fennel seeds by hand. Blend the hazelnuts and sunflower seeds in a food processor to a roughly chopped consistency. Mix in a bowl with the crushed spices, then set aside. This should yield about 200 g/1 1/2 cups of dukkah.

To serve, spoon the broccoli and buckwheat mix onto individual plates, drizzle over the dressing and cover each serving with a tablespoon of the dukkah topping.

Pearl Barley, Roast Pumpkin & Green Bean Salad

Pearl barley is great in salads, as it manages to retain a bit of texture and is one of the rare white ingredients, which makes it very useful for improving your salad aesthetics. When it comes to green beans in salads, it is absolutely essential that they are cooked correctly.

500 g/1 lb. 2 oz. pumpkin, peeled, deseeded and cut into 3-cm/1¼-in. cubes

olive oil

200 g/generous 1 cup pearl barley

400 g/14 oz. green beans, topped but not tailed

100 g/3½ oz. sun-dried tomatoes, roughly chopped

20 stoned/pitted black olives

1 tablespoon capers, drained

1 red onion, sliced

1 bunch of fresh basil, roughly chopped

1 garlic clove, crushed

sea salt and freshly ground black pepper

Serves 4-6

Preheat the oven to 200°C (400°F) Gas 6.

Toss the pumpkin with a little olive oil and salt in a roasting pan. Roast for 20–25 minutes, until soft but not disintegrating.

In the meantime, bring a pan of salted water to the boil and cook the pearl barley for about 20–30 minutes. You want the grains to be al dente, but not chalky or overly chewy. When they're ready, drain them and set aside.

For the beans, bring another pan of salted water to the boil and prepare a bowl of iced water. Add the beans and cook for 3–5 minutes. Test them by giving them a bend; you want them to be flexible but still have a nice snap if you push them too far. Once cooked, drain them and drop them immediately into the iced water. This 'refreshing' process will halt the cooking process and help keep the beans perfectly cooked and vibrantly green.

To assemble the salad, mix the pearl barley with the sun-dried tomatoes, olives, capers, red onion, basil and garlic. Add this to the roast pumpkin and green beans and stir gently until well combined. Drizzle with a little olive oil and serve.

Pearl Barley Tabbouleh

The traditional bulgur wheat in this recipe has been replaced with pearl barley, which give a delicious nuttiness of flavour. The Middle Eastern spiced tomatoes are the star of the show and make this a spectacular dish.

100 g/¹/₂ cup pearl barley

500 ml/2 cups vegetable stock

grated zest of 1 lemon

a small bunch of fresh mint

2 large bunches of fresh
  flat-leaf parsley

300 g/10¹/₂ oz. firm tomatoes,
  finely chopped

freshly squeezed juice of
  2 lemons

1 teaspoon white wine vinegar

a pinch of freshly ground
  black pepper

a pinch of ground allspice

a pinch of ground coriander

a pinch of ground cinnamon

olive oil, to drizzle

sea salt, to season

1 crusty sourdough loaf, sliced,
  or flatbreads, to serve

Serves 4

Put the barley in a large saucepan, cover with the stock and add a generous pinch of salt. Bring to the boil, then immediately take off the heat, add the lemon zest and leave to cool. The barley should absorb all of the liquid and be firm but not hard.

Leaving a handful of the mint and parsley leaves for dressing the dish, finely chop the parsley leaves and stems and the mint leaves. Add them to the cooled barley and stir through.

Put the tomatoes in a separate bowl and add the lemon juice and white wine vinegar. Add the black pepper, allspice, coriander and cinnamon, and toss to combine. Taste the salad and add a little more of the spices if you prefer it more heavily spiced.

To serve, spoon the pearl barley onto plates, then the tomatoes. Sprinkle with the reserved mint and parsley leaves and drizzle a good glug of olive oil over the top. Enjoy with slices of crusty sourdough or flatbreads.

Beetroot, Quinoa & Green Bean Salad with Spicy Ginger Dressing

2 raw beetroot/beets, skin on

a large handful of green beans, trimmed

100 g/1 cup quinoa

250 ml/1 cup vegetable stock

a handful of toasted pistachios

200 g/1½ cups canned (drained) chickpeas

2 oranges, peeled and sliced into thin rounds

FOR THE SHALLOT CRISPS

1 shallot, thinly sliced

3 tablespoons seasoned gram/chickpea flour

vegetable oil, for frying

FOR THE SPICY GINGER DRESSING

grated zest and freshly squeezed juice of ½ orange

freshly squeezed juice of ½ lemon

1 garlic clove, crushed

2-cm/¾-in. piece of fresh ginger, finely chopped or grated

½–1 red chilli/chile, deseeded and finely diced

a handful of fresh mint, finely chopped

sea salt and freshly ground black pepper

Serves 2–4

Quinoa is a great addition to a vegetarian diet as it is a complete protein source and very rich in fibre. For an extra crunchy texture, sprinkle the salad with shallot crisps.

Preheat the oven to 200°C (400°F) Gas 6.

Wrap the beetroot/beets in foil and roast them in the preheated oven for 30 minutes until they have begun to soften. Leave to cool and then cut into bite-sized pieces.

Bring a saucepan of water to the boil and cook the green beans for about 4 minutes until they are just cooked but still have a bite to them. Once the beans are cooked, plunge them into a bowl of cold water to stop the cooking process.

Put the quinoa and vegetable stock in a saucepan. Bring to the boil, then simmer for 15 minutes until the grains are cooked and the stock has been absorbed. Remove from the heat, cover the pan and let the quinoa steam for 5 minutes, then fluff with a fork.

To make the shallot crisps, toss the shallot slices in the gram/chickpea flour until well coasted. Put 1 cm/1/2 inch of oil in a deep pan or wok and set over medium-high heat. Do not allow the oil to become so hot that it smokes and spits. Drop the coated shallot slices into the oil and fry for 30 seconds until they are crisp and golden. Drain on paper towels and sprinkle with salt.

To make the dressing, put all the ingredients in a bowl and whisk until well incorporated. Season with salt and pepper.

To assemble the salad, put all the ingredients into a large bowl. Toss with the dressing, then serve on plates with a sprinkling of shallot crisps.

Winter Salad of Pearl Barley, Mushrooms & Walnuts

Pearl barley is a great, high-fibre, high-protein alternative to staples such as rice and couscous and has a lovely nutty flavour. A mix of seasonal mushrooms will give this salad a rich, earthy taste, while the chilli/chile adds a welcome touch of warming spice on a cold day.

200 g/1 cup pearl barley

400 ml/1²/₃ cups vegetable stock

a handful of walnut halves

1 tablespoon walnut oil

320 g/about 5 cups sliced mixed seasonal mushrooms

2 garlic cloves, crushed

¼ teaspoon dried rosemary

¼ teaspoon dried chilli/hot red pepper flakes

a handful of peppery salad leaves

sea salt and freshly ground black pepper

FOR THE VINAIGRETTE DRESSING

4 spring onions/scallions, finely chopped

2 tablespoons walnut oil

2 teaspoons balsamic vinegar

a squeeze of lemon juice

a handful of fresh flat-leaf parsley, finely chopped

Serves 2–4

Put the pearl barley and stock in a saucepan set over a medium heat. Bring to the boil, then simmer for 20–30 minutes until it is tender but retains its bite.

Meanwhile, toast the walnuts in a dry frying pan/skillet set over a medium heat until they start to brown then remove from the heat.

Heat the walnut oil in a separate frying pan/skillet and add the mushrooms and garlic. Fry until golden, then season with salt and pepper. Stir in the rosemary and dried chilli/hot red pepper flakes. Pour the mixture into a heatproof bowl and put the pan back on the hob to make the dressing.

To make the dressing, put the spring onions/scallions, walnut oil, balsamic vinegar and lemon juice in the pan and stir until well combined. Set the pan over a low heat and cook until the mixture bubbles. Remove from the heat, season with salt and pepper and stir in the parsley.

To assemble the salad, put the salad leaves in a large bowl with the mushrooms, toasted walnuts and pearl barley and add the dressing. Toss to combine, spoon into serving bowls and serve immediately.

BEANS & PULSES

Three Beans with Mint & Lime

This bean and mint salad is extra special if the beans are home-grown as there is so much pleasure in growing your own.

175 g/1 cup broad/fava beans, shelled

150 g/1 cup runner beans, sliced

150 g/1 cup French beans

1 small red onion, finely chopped

grated zest and freshly squeezed juice of 2 limes

2 tablespoons olive oil

a generous handful of fresh mint leaves, roughly chopped

sea salt and freshly ground black pepper

Serves 4

Cook all the beans together in a pan of salted, boiling water, until al dente – approximately 4 minutes. Drain and refresh with cold water.

Dress the beans with the finely chopped onion and lime zest. Mix the olive oil and lime juice together in a small bowl and season well with salt and pepper. Pour the dressing over the bean salad when you are ready to serve and scatter over the mint.

Warm Lentil Salad with Marinated Cow's Milk Feta

This salad is absolutely divine stuffed into warm pitta breads or simply served in a bowl.

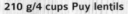

210 g/4 cups Puy lentils

1 small red (bell) pepper, cut into 1-cm/½-in. strips

1 small yellow (bell) pepper, cut into 1-cm/½-in. strips

2 tablespoons olive oil

2 garlic cloves, crushed

2.5-cm/1-in. piece of fresh ginger, peeled and very finely chopped

1 teaspoon ground cumin

½ –¾ teaspoon ground coriander

2 tablespoons pine nuts, lightly toasted in a dry pan

10 cherry tomatoes, halved

275 g/2 cups marinated cow's milk feta, cubed

sea salt and freshly ground black pepper

FOR THE SALAD DRESSING

75 ml/½ cup olive oil

2 tablespoons red wine vinegar

6 g/¼ cup freshly chopped mint

grated zest of 3 lemons and freshly squeezed juice of 2 lemons

Serves 6–8

Preheat the oven to 200°C (400°F) Gas 6.

Put the lentils in a medium saucepan and cover with cold water. Bring to the boil. Reduce the heat and simmer until tender (about 25 minutes). Drain well and set aside.

Put the (bell) peppers onto a baking sheet, coat with 1 tablespoon of the olive oil and season with salt and pepper. Roast the peppers in the preheated oven for 7–10 minutes until tender. Set aside.

Heat the remaining oil in a small frying pan/skillet. Add the garlic and ginger and sauté gently for 1 minute. Remove the pan from the heat, add the cumin and coriander and stir well. Set aside.

Put the pine nuts in a dry frying pan/skillet and lightly toast over a medium heat, stirring frequently, until golden. Remove and set aside.

To make the dressing, combine the olive oil, vinegar, mint and lemon zest and juice in a serving bowl.

Add the lentils, (bell) peppers, half the pine nuts, the cherry tomatoes, half the feta and seasoning to the serving bowl and mix together to combine.

Scatter over the remaining pine nuts and feta and serve.

Mushroom, Goat's Cheese & Lentil Salad

When you don't want to spend too long in the kitchen, this is ideal. It draws on storecupboard staples – lentils, olive oil, mustard and vinegar – to create a tasty meal. Adding raw mushrooms, soft, tangy goat's cheese, fresh herbs and lemon zest gives a lovely lift to the whole dish, making it perfect for warm-weather eating.

100 g/½ cup Puy/French green lentils

3 tablespoons olive oil, plus extra for serving

1 tablespoon balsamic or red wine vinegar

1 teaspoon Dijon mustard

1–2 sprigs of fresh parsley, finely chopped

250 g/8 oz. white/cup mushrooms, sliced 5 mm/ ¼-in. thick

150 g/5½ oz. soft goat's cheese, crumbled

2 tablespoons freshly chopped mint leaves

grated zest of 1 lemon

sea salt and freshly ground black pepper

Serves 4

Rinse the lentils, then place in a saucepan and cover generously with cold water. Bring to the boil, then reduce the heat and simmer for 25 minutes until tender; drain.

While the lentils are cooking, mix together the olive oil, vinegar and mustard and season with salt and pepper. Toss the warm lentils with the dressing, then set aside to cool.

Toss the lentils with the parsley and place in a salad serving bowl. Top with the mushrooms and goat's cheese. Sprinkle with the mint and lemon zest. Dress with a little more olive oil and serve at once.

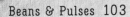

Broad Bean & Pea Salad with Sourdough Croutons & Tarragon

This salad is full of summer promise. Why not take it outside and serve it alongside some freshly baked bread?

250 g/9 oz. podded broad/fava beans or butter/lima beans

200 g/7 oz. podded fresh peas

3 slices of sourdough bread, ideally a little dry

1–2 tablespoons olive oil

2 Little Gem lettuces or several handfuls of Cos/Romaine lettuce

FOR THE DRESSING

4 tablespoons crème fraîche or soured cream

2 teaspoons Dijon mustard

grated zest and freshly squeezed juice of 1 unwaxed lemon

1 garlic clove, crushed

6 tablespoons olive oil, plus extra for drizzling

40 g/1/3 cup freshly grated Parmesan cheese, plus extra shavings for scattering

2 generous handfuls of fresh tarragon, chopped, plus extra leaves for scattering

sea salt and freshly ground black pepper

Serves 4–6

Bring some water to the boil in a medium pan. Add some salt and the beans and cook them for 5 minutes. Refresh the beans with cold water, drain them well and remove the skins to reveal their vibrant green flesh (if using broad/fava beans).

If the peas are young and sweet, they can be served raw. If not, cook them for 3 minutes in boiling water, then refresh in cold water to prevent them cooking further, and drain well.

Cut the bread into fork-friendly squares and heat the olive oil in a frying pan/skillet. Fry the bread pieces until golden all over, then set aside.

For the dressing, combine the crème fraîche or soured cream with the mustard, lemon zest and juice and garlic, season with salt and pepper and slowly whisk in the olive oil until you have a thick, unctuous dressing. Add the grated Parmesan cheese. The thickness of the dressing should be that of double/heavy cream. Add a little water to slacken it, if necessary.

Add the chopped tarragon to the dressing. Tear the lettuce and toss with the beans, peas, dressing and half the croutons.

Scatter with the remaining croutons, tarragon leaves and Parmesan shavings. Drizzle the salad with a little more olive oil before serving.

Georgian Red Bean Salad with Walnuts & Pomegranate Seeds

Red beans, walnuts and pomegranates are a familiar sight in the markets of Georgia, a fascinating country at the crossroads of Europe and Asia. The visual contrast of deep red beans, sparkling pomegranate seeds and bright green herbs make this a handsome salad for autumn/fall.

2 tablespoons walnut, olive or sunflower/safflower oil

1 tablespoon pomegranate molasses

250 g/1¼ cups cooked, soaked dried red kidney beans, or 1 x 400-g/14-oz. can

50 g/⅓ cup shelled walnuts

1 garlic clove, peeled

1 tablespoon white wine vinegar

a small bunch of fresh flat-leaf parsley, coriander/cilantro and mint leaves, roughly chopped

½ teaspoon ground coriander

½ teaspoon ground cinnamon

a pinch of ground cloves

1 pomegranate

½ teaspoon freshly ground black pepper or cayenne pepper

sea salt

Serves 4

Whisk together the oil and pomegranate molasses in a bowl to make a dressing. Warm the beans in their cooking or canning liquid, then drain and toss them in the dressing. Set aside.

Grind or finely chop half of the walnuts and the garlic clove – be careful not to reduce them to a sticky paste if using an electric grinder – and mix in the vinegar. Add this, together with the chopped herbs and spices, to the beans and stir well to distribute all of the ingredients evenly. Season to taste with salt and the black or cayenne pepper.

Toast the remaining walnuts for a couple of minutes in a dry frying pan/skillet, then allow to cool and roughly chop.

Next, remove the seeds from the pomegranate. The easiest way to do this is to cut the fruit into quarters, roll back the segments to expose the seeds, then push the seeds into a bowl, picking out any bits of membrane as you go.

Mix the pomegranate seeds into the salad, strew the toasted chopped walnuts over and serve.

Black Bean Salad with Avocado & Lime

The Aztecs were already eating guacamole at the time of the Spanish Conquest, and the winning combination of avocado, chilli/chile, tomato and coriander/cilantro leaves, laced with lime, now rivals hummus in its universal popularity. By chopping the avocado instead of mashing it, and stirring in some cooked black beans, you have a salad with a distinctly Mexican flavour, which is equally irresistible.

grated zest and freshly
squeezed juice of 1 lime

3 tablespoons olive oil

2 green chillies/chiles,
deseeded and finely chopped

1 tablespoon freshly chopped
coriander/cilantro

1 tablespoon freshly chopped
mint

a pinch of sugar (optional)

250 g/1¼ cups cooked, soaked
dried black beans, drained,
or the contents of 1 x 400-g/
14-oz. can, drained and rinsed

2 ripe avocados, peeled,
stoned/pitted and chopped

250 g/9 oz. cherry tomatoes,
cut in half

2 spring onions/scallions,
trimmed and finely chopped

sea salt and freshly ground
black pepper

Serves 4

Put the lime zest and juice into a bowl. Whisk in the olive oil until the dressing emulsifies. Season with salt and pepper, then stir in the chillies/chiles and chopped fresh herbs. Taste the dressing, and if it seems too sharp, add a little bit of sugar.

Put the beans, avocados, tomatoes and spring onions/scallions into a large bowl and pour the dressing over. Toss everything together until all the ingredients are combined, and serve.

Puy Lentils with Roasted Beetroot

If a fishy taste appeals, add some fish sauce to the dressing instead of salt. Serve the salad on its own, or strewn with crumbled salty cheese, such as feta, or slices of grilled halloumi cheese.

500 g/1 lb. beetroot/beets, peeled and cut into wedges

3 tablespoons olive oil

3 fresh or dried bay leaves

1 sprig of fresh thyme or 1 teaspoon dried thyme

200 g/1 cup dried Puy/French green lentils, rinsed and drained

2 garlic cloves, peeled but left whole

3 tablespoons freshly chopped flat-leaf parsley

2 tablespoons freshly chopped fresh mint

sea salt and freshly ground black pepper

FOR THE DRESSING

1 tablespoon balsamic vinegar

1 tablespoon maple syrup

2 tablespoons freshly squeezed lemon juice

2 tablespoons olive oil

Serves 4-6

Preheat the oven to 180°C (350°F) Gas 4.

Place the beetroot/beets in a small roasting pan, and toss in 2 tablespoons of the olive oil together with 3 tablespoons of water, 2 of the bay leaves and the thyme. Season with salt and pepper, cover with foil and roast in the preheated oven until they are soft – about 1 hour.

Meanwhile, boil the lentils in a saucepan of water, together with the whole garlic cloves and the remaining bay leaf and olive oil, for about 30 minutes, or until thoroughly cooked.

Whisk all the ingredients for the dressing together.

Drain the lentils and stir in all but 1 tablespoon of the dressing and all the chopped fresh herbs. Arrange the chunks of cooked beetroot/beets over, drizzle with the remaining dressing and serve at room temperature.

Warm Curried Lentil Salad with Paneer or Tofu & Spiced Dressing

400-g/14-oz. can green lentils

2 sticks celery, finely sliced

2 carrots, grated

50 g/heaped 1/3 cup cashews, toasted

1/2 mango, peeled, stoned/pitted, cut in half and thinly sliced lengthways

finely grated zest of 1/2 lime

1 tablespoon vegetable oil

200 g/7 oz. paneer or tofu, sliced

a handful of fresh mint or coriander/cilantro leaves, chopped

lime wedges, to serve

FOR THE SPICED DRESSING

4 tablespoons vegetable oil

1 shallot, finely chopped

1/2 teaspoon mustard seeds

1 teaspoon garam masala

1/2 teaspoon ground turmeric

a pinch of dried chilli/hot red pepper flakes

1 garlic clove, crushed

1 teaspoon sugar

1 tablespoon white wine vinegar

50 g/1/3 cup sultanas/golden raisins

1/2 red chilli/chile, deseeded and finely diced

Serves 2–4

This fresh and tasty salad is mildly spiced and perfect with either fried paneer, or marinated tofu for a vegan version. The salad itself keeps well so can be made in advance, allowing the flavours to develop.

To make the spiced dressing, heat half the vegetable oil in a small saucepan. Add the shallot and cook over a low heat for 5 minutes, until it starts to soften but still has a slight bite and has not taken on any colour. Add the remaining oil, the mustard seeds, garam masala, turmeric, dried chilli/hot red pepper flakes, garlic and sugar, and cook for 2 minutes. Turn off the heat and add the vinegar, sultanas/golden raisins and red chilli/chile.

For the salad, put the lentils, celery, carrots, toasted cashews, mango and lime zest in a large bowl. Pour in the warm dressing, reserving about 2 tablespoons to serve, and stir until well combined and coated in the dressing.

To cook the paneer or tofu, heat the vegetable oil in a frying pan/skillet and fry the slices until golden on both sides, using tongs to turn them halfway through cooking.

Brush the paneer or tofu slices with the reserved dressing and serve on top of the salad. Finish the salad with chopped mint or coriander/cilantro, and with lime wedges on the side for squeezing.

Mushroom & Seaweed Noodle Salad

With its Japanese-inspired combination of subtle flavours and textures, this makes a stylish noodle dish, served at room temperature and ideal for either lunch or dinner. For maximum visual impact, use as varied a mixture of fresh exotic mushrooms as you can find.

175 g/6 oz. egg noodles or soba noodles

200 g/7 oz. assorted exotic mushrooms (shiitake, eryngii, oyster, shiro shimeji)

10 g/¼ oz. dried wakame, soaked in warm water for 5 minutes, then drained

75 g/⅔ cup frozen edamame/ soya beans, cooked and drained

a thumb-sized piece of fresh ginger, peeled and grated

1 spring onion/scallion, finely chopped, white and green parts separated

1 tablespoon sesame seeds, plus extra for serving

FOR THE DRESSING

100 ml/6 tablespoons dashi stock

2 tablespoons mirin

3 tablespoons light soy sauce

1 tablespoon sesame oil

Serves 4

Cook the noodles according to the packet instructions until al dente; drain and then plunge into cold water. Drain once more.

Trim the assorted mushrooms, slicing any larger ones.

Mix together all the dressing ingredients in a small bowl.

Toss together the cooked noodles, wakame, edamame/ soya beans, fresh ginger, whites of the spring onion/ scallion and the dressing in a serving bowl. Toss with the sesame seeds. Toss two-thirds of the mushrooms through the noodles. Top with the remaining mushrooms, sprinkle with the green spring onion/scallion and serve at once.

Greek Salad with Butter Beans

This is a slight twist on a classic Greek salad. Butter/lima beans are a staple of Greek cuisine but are usually served baked in a rich tomato sauce. Their delicate flavour works well here with tangy feta and olives.

400 g/2 cups cherry tomatoes, halved

50 g/½ cup kalamata olives, halved and stoned/pitted

leaves from a small bunch of fresh mint, roughly chopped

leaves from a small bunch of flat-leaf parsley, finely chopped

2 x 400-g/14-oz. cans butter/lima beans, drained and rinsed

3 tablespoons olive oil

2 red onions, thinly sliced

2 garlic cloves, finely chopped

3 tablespoons freshly squeezed lemon juice

200 g/heaped 1½ cups feta cheese, cut into cubes

sea salt and freshly ground black pepper

bread, to serve

Serves 4

Put the tomatoes, olives, mint, parsley and beans in a large bowl and toss to combine.

Put the olive oil in a frying pan/skillet set over a medium heat. Add the onions and garlic. When they start to sizzle in the oil, remove from the heat and pour over the tomato mixture. Stir in the lemon juice and add the feta. Season to taste with salt and pepper and toss well to combine. Serve at room temperature with bread.

CHEESE

Tomato, Melon & Feta Salad

Perfect food for hot-weather dining. Sweet melon combined with juicy tomatoes and contrasted with salty feta, makes this a lovely dish. For a saltier contrast, substitute the feta with blue cheese. Serve with crusty bread to mop up every last drop of deliciousness.

½ cantaloupe melon, peeled, deseeded and diced

½ Galia or other green-fleshed melon, peeled, deseeded and diced

300 g/10½ oz. tomatoes, sliced into wedges

2 tablespoons extra virgin olive oil

1 tablespoon sherry vinegar

2 tablespoons freshly chopped chives

100 g/3½ oz. feta cheese, diced

freshly ground black pepper

Serves 4

Toss together all the melon and tomato pieces with the oil, vinegar and chives in a serving dish. Season well with pepper.

Gently mix in the feta cheese and serve at once.

Sun-blush Tomato, Orange & Burrata Salad

Gloriously simple to put together, this bright and colourful dish offers a Mediterranean-inspired combination of colours, textures and flavours.

2 large oranges

24 sun-blush/semi-dried cherry tomato halves

2 burrata cheeses (or good-quality fresh mozzarella cheese)

TO SERVE

olive oil

freshly ground black pepper

a handful of fresh basil leaves

Serves 4

Peel the oranges, making sure to trim off all the white pith, and cut into even, thick slices.

Place the orange slices on a large serving dish, then scatter over the sun-blush/semi-dried tomato halves. Tear the burrata cheeses into chunks and layer on top of the orange slices and tomato halves.

Drizzle with olive oil and season with pepper. Garnish with the basil leaves and serve at once.

Black Garlic Tricolore Salad

Insalata tricolore – Italy's patriotic red, white and green salad – is a classic which, when made with good-quality tomatoes, ripe avocado and fresh mozzarella, is such a treat to eat. Adding black garlic is an unorthodox touch, but the smoky sweetness of black garlic works well with the balsamic vinegar and gives an interesting flavour to the dish.

3 mozzarella cheese balls, drained and sliced

4 ripe tomatoes, sliced

2 ripe avocados, peeled, stoned/pitted, sliced and tossed with a little lemon juice to prevent discolouring

a handful of fresh basil leaves

sea salt and freshly ground black pepper

FOR THE DRESSING

6 tablespoons olive oil

2 tablespoons balsamic vinegar

2 black garlic cloves, finely chopped

Serves 4

Make the dressing by placing the olive oil, balsamic vinegar and black garlic in a small lidded jar, then shaking well to mix together. Season with salt and pepper.

Arrange the mozzarella, tomato and avocado slices overlapping on a large serving plate. Pour over the black garlic dressing, scatter over the basil leaves and serve at once.

Pea Shoot, Endive, Provolone, Pear & Walnut Salad

Provolone is a cow's milk cheese from Italy's southern region. It has a slightly smoky flavour and fine texture. The colour is pale yellow when aged between two and three months, but as the cheese ripens, the colour and flavour deepen. A mature goat's cheese would also work very well in this salad.

100 g/1 cup fresh walnut halves

1 head chicory/Belgian endive

½ head radicchio

a handful of fresh basil, torn

a handful of mint, chopped

125 g/4½ oz. pea shoots

2 large, ripe but firm pears (Williams are good)

150 g/5½ oz. Provolone cheese, cut into triangles

FOR THE VINAIGRETTE

1 tablespoon red wine vinegar

2 teaspoons aged balsamic vinegar

3 tablespoons walnut oil

1 tablespoon olive oil

sea salt and freshly ground black pepper

Serves 4-6

Preheat the oven to 180°C (350°F) Gas 4.

Spread the walnuts on a baking sheet and bake them for 10 minutes until they are fragrant. Let cool before roughly chopping.

Next, make the vinaigrette. Combine the salt, red wine vinegar and balsamic vinegar in a bowl and whisk until the salt has dissolved. Trickle in the two types of oil, whisking all the while until the mixture has emulsified. Season to taste with pepper.

Separate the chicory/endive and radicchio leaves, rinse well and pat dry. Place in a bowl with the herbs and pea shoots. Add 2 tablespoons of the vinaigrette and toss well, then use to make a bed on a plate.

Quarter and core the pears, then arrange them on top of the leaves with the cheese and walnuts. Drizzle with the dressing and serve straight away.

Portobello Mushroom & Chèvre Salad

Marinated raw mushrooms combined with mild, fresh goat's cheese and a handful of salad leaves make a complete protein-rich meal that will leave you satisfied.

4 big Portobello mushrooms or 8 smaller ones

300 g/10½ oz. chèvre (goat's cheese), unpasteurized if available

150–200 g/4–5 cups lamb's lettuce/corn salad, or other salad leaves

4–6 tablespoons olive oil

apple cider vinegar, to taste

FOR THE MUSHROOM MARINADE

2 tablespoons tamari

1 tablespoon olive oil

1 garlic clove, crushed

1 tablespoon freshly squeezed lemon juice

freshly ground black pepper

Serves 4

For the mushroom marinade, combine all the ingredients in a small bowl and season with salt and pepper.

Wipe the mushrooms with paper towels and cut away any dark spots on either the caps or stems. Cut the mushrooms into 5-mm/¼-inch-thick slices and put in a shallow bowl. Pour the marinade over them, mix well and refrigerate for anything from 1 up to 24 hours. The mushroom flesh will soften, soak up the marinade and wilt a little, which is all good.

When you are ready to serve the salad, cut the chèvre into cubes or thick slices. Wash the salad, drain well and pat dry.

Put the marinated mushrooms, chèvre and salad in a salad bowl. Add the olive oil, a dash of vinegar and some pepper, to taste. Mix well.

Serve the salad with your choice of crackers or bread.

You can add Mediterranean dried herbs to this salad too, such as oregano, basil, rosemary, etc., if you like.

Buffalo Mozzarella with Peperonata & Rosemary Ciabatta Croutons

100 ml/⅓ cup olive oil, plus extra for the croutons

3 garlic cloves

1 red onion, sliced

2 red (bell) peppers, sliced into 1-cm/½-in. strips

2 yellow (bell) peppers, sliced into 1-cm/½-in. strips

2 bay leaves

2 plum tomatoes, deseeded and cut into chunks

1 tablespoon red wine vinegar

½ teaspoon sea salt

½ teaspoon sugar

1 tablespoon capers, drained

a handful of cherry tomatoes, halved

a bunch of fresh basil

small ciabatta loaf

2 sprigs of fresh rosemary, leaves finely chopped

4 balls buffalo mozzarella, about 150 g/5 oz. each, halved

sea salt and freshly ground black pepper

rocket/arugula leaves, to serve

a handful of toasted pine nuts

Serves 6–8

The combination of creamy white mozzarella and robust, oily peperonata is a sight to behold. The only thing the combination lacks is crunch, which is where the ciabatta croutons come in.

Heat a deep frying pan/skillet over a medium heat. Add the olive oil and garlic. Fry the garlic on both sides until golden brown, then remove from the pan and set aside. Add the red onion and cook, stirring frequently, until it is pale and translucent but not yet brown. Add the (bell) peppers, fried garlic and bay leaves. Cover and cook for 15 minutes or so, until the (bell) peppers are soft but still holding their shape.

Remove the lid and add the diced tomatoes, vinegar, salt and sugar. Cook, uncovered, for a further 10 minutes, then add the capers and cherry tomatoes and take off the heat. The residual heat in the peperonata will soften the cherry tomatoes, but not cook them to a mush. Leave to cool, then add the basil and season with salt and pepper, if necessary.

For the rosemary ciabatta croutons, preheat the oven to 200°C (400°F) Gas 6. Slice the ciabatta on the diagonal as thinly as you can. Mix the rosemary with some olive oil and brush it generously onto the ciabatta slices. You want the bread well coated in oil. Season with salt and bake on a wire rack in the preheated oven for 5–8 minutes, until golden brown and crisp.

Serve the buffalo mozzarella on a bed of rocket/arugula and the peperonata, with the ciabatta croutons and pine nuts scattered around.

Roasted Butternut Squash, Beetroot & Goat's Cheese Salad

This is a solid, chunky salad that can be prepared well in advance.

4 raw beetroot/beets, ideally 2 red and 2 golden

50 ml/¼ cup clear honey

1 medium butternut squash, peeled, deseeded and cut into wedges

olive oil, for roasting

2 sprigs of fresh rosemary, chopped

200 g/7 oz. goat's cheese (the log variety works best here)

½ bunch of freshly chopped flat-leaf parsley

finely grated zest of 1 unwaxed lemon

50 g/⅔ cup flaked/sliced almonds

sea salt and freshly ground black pepper

baby spinach leaves or rocket/arugula, to serve

an ovenproof roasting pan, oiled

Serves 4

Preheat the oven to 200°C (400°F) Gas 6.

Put the beetroot/beets into a pan with tepid water and bring to the boil. If you're using both the red and golden types, be sure to cook them separately or the gold colour will get cannibalized by the red. Cook them for approximately 45 minutes. Test them by inserting a knife; if the point goes in easily with little or no resistance, remove and drain in a colander. Run cold water over them and peel while still hot, as the skin comes off much more easily this way.

Cut the beetroot/beets into wedges and place them in the oiled roasting pan. Season generously with salt and pepper and drizzle with the honey.

In a separate roasting pan, mix the butternut squash with a splash of olive oil and the rosemary, and season well.

Put the beetroot/beets and butternut squash in the oven and roast for 45 minutes, or until golden brown. Remove and allow them to cool until you can handle them.

Remove the rind from the goat's cheese and crumble the cheese. Mix the roasted vegetables with the parsley, goats' cheese, lemon zest and almonds. Serve on a bed of baby spinach or rocket/arugula.

Smoked Parsnip, Pear & Stilton Salad

This marriage of traditional English flavours makes a delightful light warm salad. Have fun making a simple home smoker and experiment with smoking other ingredients; root vegetables take smoke very well.

300 g/10½ oz. parsnips, peeled and sliced lengthways

vegetable oil, for coating and frying

2 just-ripe pears, peeled and cut lengthways into quarters, seeds removed

1 chicory/Belgian endive, trimmed into leaves

100 g/1 cup walnut halves

1 teaspoon runny honey or agave syrup

100 g/3½ oz. Stilton or hard blue cheese

sea salt

FOR THE SMOKE

1 tablespoon white sugar

2 tablespoons white rice

2 tablespoons loose Earl Grey tea leaves

Serves 4

Preheat the oven to 180°C (350°F) Gas 4.

Lightly tea-smoke the parsnips following the method below for 5 minutes. Once smoked, rub them with vegetable oil. Put in a roasting pan and roast in the preheated oven for 20 minutes.

Add a little vegetable oil to a frying pan/skillet and set over a medium heat. Add the pears, chicory/Belgian endive leaves and walnuts. Cook for about 5 minutes, turning regularly to cook evenly. Remove from the heat, drizzle with the honey or agave syrup and turn the ingredients gently in the pan, coating them in the pan juices and adding just a hint of honey/syrup flavour. Sprinkle with a good pinch of salt to season.

Serve the smoked parsnips and the pan-fried pears, walnuts and chicory/Belgian endive on warm plates. Crumble the Stilton into bite-sized pieces and scatter around the salad.

Home smoking: To make a smoker, put the sugar, rice and Earl Grey tea in the base of a wok. Cover the mixture with two layers of foil, with a piece of crumpled foil between the layers, making a gap of about 1 cm/½ inch. This will allow the smoke to seep around the edges of the foil.

Set the wok over a high heat. Rest the parsnips (or other vegetables) on top of the foil and cover the wok with a lid. Leave to smoke for 5 minutes. Once smoked, finish cooking the parsnips according to the recipe above.

Roast Butternut Squash & Four Cheese Salad

You can serve the butternut squash and hazelnuts made in this recipe hot, straight from the oven for a rich and intense flavour, or cold.

1 butternut squash, peeled, deseeded and diced into 2-cm/³/₄-in. pieces

vegetable oil, to coat

150 g/1 cup blanched hazelnuts

200 g/7 oz. Cheddar cheese, diced into 5-mm/¼-in. pieces

150 g/5¹/₂ oz. blue cheese, crumbled

115 g/4 oz. mozzarella cheese, cut into bite-sized pieces

100 g/1¹/₃ cups grated Parmesan cheese

12 dandelion leaves (available in health food stores, at farmers' markets or online), finely chopped

70 g/3 cups rocket/arugula

70 g/3 cups mixed lettuce leaves

sea salt

FOR THE VINAIGRETTE

250 ml/1 cup olive oil

100 ml/¹/₃ cup white wine vinegar

1 tablespoon runny honey

2 teaspoons Dijon mustard

Serves 4

To make the vinaigrette, add all the ingredients to a food processor and blitz for a couple of minutes. Set aside for an hour.

Preheat the oven to 180°C (350°F) Gas 4.

Toss the butternut squash in some vegetable oil with the hazelnuts and a generous pinch of salt. Transfer to a baking sheet and bake in the preheated oven for 10–15 minutes, or until the butternut squash has softened and the hazelnuts are starting to brown.

Put the Cheddar, blue cheese and mozzarella into a large mixing bowl, add the vinaigrette, sprinkle the Parmesan over the top and toss to combine.

Add the dandelion leaves to the cheese mixture and stir gently. Add the rocket/arugula and lettuce leaves and gently toss the salad to combine the cheeses and leaves together. The leaves should have a light coating of the vinaigrette but add more if you prefer.

Spoon the salad onto four plates and scatter the baked butternut squash and hazelnuts over the top to serve.

Caesar Salad

This salad was invented during the prohibition era by chef Caesar Cardini (of Italian descent) in Tijuana, Mexico, for American tourists.

200 ml/³/₄ cup olive oil,
  plus extra to drizzle

2 garlic cloves, crushed

4 slices sourdough bread,
  cut into 1-cm/¹/₂-in. cubes

2 Cos/Romaine lettuce heads,
  halved lengthways

freshly squeezed juice
  of ¹/₂ lemon

1 egg yolk

100 g/3¹/₂ oz. Parmesan cheese

Worcestershire sauce, to taste

Serves 4

First, make the garlic oil. Heat the olive oil and crushed garlic in a pan to over 85°C (185°F), then remove from the heat and leave to cool for at least an hour, while the flavours infuse.

Preheat the oven to 180°C (350°F) Gas 4.

Toss the sourdough cubes in the garlic oil until evenly coated. Spread out on a baking sheet and cook in the preheated oven for 20 minutes or until golden. Once removed from the oven, they will continue to crisp up even more as they cool.

Drizzle a little olive oil over the cut surface of the lettuce heads. Preheat a stove-top griddle/grill pan over a high heat and place the lettuce cut-side down in the pan. Cook for a few minutes until just starting to blacken.

To make the salad dressing, put the garlic oil, lemon juice and egg yolk in a jar with a screw-top lid, tighten the lid and shake to combine.

To serve, arrange the lettuce halves, cut-side up, on plates. Finely grate half of the Parmesan over the top – it should begin to melt. Sprinkle the croutons over the plates.

Dress the salad generously with the salad dressing, then drizzle with a little Worcestershire sauce and shave the remaining Parmesan over the top before serving.

Roasted Vegetable Salad with Grilled Halloumi, Rocket & Basil Oil

A fresh and colourful salad that is quick and easy to prepare – perfect for a mid-week meal. Simply chop your preferred vegetables and roast them in the oven for 40–60 minutes while you put your feet up.

2 red onions, quartered

1 aubergine/eggplant, cut into chunks

1 courgette/zucchini, cut into chunks

1 sweet potato, cut into chunks

1 red bell pepper, sliced into strips

a handful of cherry tomatoes

4 garlic cloves, unpeeled

3 tablespoons olive oil, plus extra for greasing

250 g/9 oz. halloumi, sliced into strips

140 g/2½ cups rocket/arugula

a small handful of toasted pine nuts

sea salt and freshly ground black pepper

FOR THE BASIL OIL

a small handful of fresh basil leaves

100 ml/⅓ cup olive oil

Serves 4

Preheat the oven to 200°C (400°F) Gas 6.

Put the vegetables and garlic in a large roasting pan with the olive oil. Season well with salt and pepper and toss to mix. Roast the vegetables in the preheated oven for 40–60 minutes, until they are soft and golden but still holding their shape.

To make the basil oil, bring a small saucepan of water to the boil. Put the basil leaves in the boiling water for just 10 seconds. Remove them and dip in a bowl of cold water to cool. Drain and dry the basil leaves, then put them in a food processor and set the motor running. Drizzle in the olive oil then strain the mixture into a bowl and set aside.

Lightly oil a stove-top griddle/grill pan or frying pan/skillet and set over medium heat. Lay the strips of halloumi in the pan and cook until they turn golden brown, turning halfway through cooking.

To assemble the salad, stir the rocket/arugula through the roasted vegetables. Spoon the salad onto a serving plate and top with the halloumi. Drizzle with the basil oil and sprinkle over the pine nuts. Serve immediately.

Index

Photography Credits

Jan Baldwin 32, 105, 126, 127

Peter Cassidy 5, 10–14, 36, 37, 66–69, 96, 103, 116, 117, 120, 121, 123

Tara Fisher 2–3, 38–41, 47, 48, 77

Richard Jung 118

David Munns 46, 99

Steve Painter 9, 29, 30, 44, 63, 90, 119, 135, 136, 139

William Reavell 1, 4, 6–8, 18, 19, 33, 34, 45, 65, 71, 78, 79, 81, 82, 93, 94, 97, 100, 106–113, 140, endpapers

Kate Whitaker 21, 25–27, 31, 51, 53, 58–60, 80, 89, 128–132, 137, 141

Clare Winfield 15, 17, 20, 22–24, 42, 43, 52, 54–57, 61, 64, 70, 72–74, 85, 86, 91, 98, 101, 102, 114, 122, 124, 125

Recipe Credits

Jordan Bourke
Camargue Red Rice Salad with Black Grapes, Pecans & Marjoram
Greek Salad with Butter Beans
Quinoa with Mint, Orange & Beetroot
Peach Panzanella
Watermelon, Black Olive & Rose Water Salad

Chloe Coker and Jane Montgomery
Asian-style Hot & Sour Salad with Marinated Tofu
Beetroot, Quinoa & Green Bean Salad with Spicy Ginger Dressing
Roasted Vegetable Salad with Grilled Halloumi Rocket & Basil Oil
Summer Vegetable Carpaccio
Warm Curried Lentil Salad with Paneer & Spiced Dressing
Winter Salad of Pearl Barley, Mushrooms & Walnuts

Ursula Ferrigno
Broad Bean & Pea Salad with Sourdough Croutons & Tarragon
Grilled Lettuce & Spelt Lemon Salad
Lemon, Fennel & Rocket Salad with Radicchio
Lemon Summer Grain Salad
Pea Shoot, Endive, Provolone, Pear & Walnut Salad
Roast Cauliflower with Almonds & Preserved Lemon
Three Beans with Mint & Lime
Warm Lentil Salad with Marinated Cow's Milk Feta

Amy Ruth Finegold
Avocado, Rocket & Grapefruit Salad with Sunflower Seeds
Quinoa Salad with Spring Vegetables & Herbs in a Citrus Dressing
Shaved Broccoli & Buckwheat Salad with Dukkah Topping
Shredded Carrot & Courgette Salad with Sesame Miso Sauce
Wheatberry Salad with Apples & Pecans
Wild Rice with Artichoke, Peaches & Pine Nuts

Mat Follas
Caesar Salad
Celeriac Remoulade with Heritage Beetroot & Fennel
Pearl Barley Tabbouleh
Pimms Salad
Roast Butternut Squash & Four Cheese Salad
Rocket, Black Olive, Feta & Orange Salad
Smoked Parsnip, Pear & Stilton Salad
Thai Tofu Salad

Acland Geddes
Buffalo Mozzarella with Peperonata & Rosemary Ciabatta Croutons
Crunchy Fennel Salad with Pomegranate, Mango & Walnuts
Grilled Courgettes with Basil, Mint & Lemon
Pearl Barley, Roast Pumpkin & Green Bean Salad
Roasted Butternut Squash, Beetroot & Goat's Cheese Salad
Raw Parsnip Salad with Curry Dressing
Red Cabbage, Beetroot, Feta & Apricot Salad

Dunja Gulin
Micro Salad with Parsley Dressing
Pearled Spelt Salad with Button Mushrooms & Watercress
Pink Quinoa Salad with Fennel & Arame
Portobello Mushroom & Chèvre Salad
Spicy & Sweet Salad with Kumquats & Brazil Nuts
Vegan Caesar Salad
Wild Rice with Rocket & Pine Nuts

Vicky Jones
Georgian Red Bean Salad with Walnuts & Pomegranate Seeds
Black Bean Salad with Avocado & Lime
Puy Lentils with Roasted Beetroot

Jenny Linford
Black Garlic Tricolore Salad
Hazelnut, Mushroom & Bulgur Wheat Salad
Heritage Tomato Fennel Salad;
Kachumber
Mushroom, Goat's Cheese & Lentil Salad
Mushroom & Seaweed Noodle Salad
Sun-blush Tomato, Orange & Burrata Salad
Thai Tomato Salad
Tomato Fattoush
Tomato, Freekah & Avocado Salad
Tomato Tabbouleh
Tomato, Melon & Feta Salad